종이인형 페이퍼 크라프트 아트북

VINTAGE PAPER DOLLS

31 SETS OF FULL COLOURED COSTUME PLATES FOR GIRLS & LADIES

클라시코 페이퍼 크라프트 01

빈티지 페이퍼돌

KB241723

CLASSICO
PAPER CRAFT

Part of Cow & Bridge Publishing Co.
Web site : www.cafe.naver.com/sowadari
3ga-302, 6-21, 40th St., Guwolro, Namgu, Incheon, #402-848 South Korea
Telephone 0505-719-7787 Facsimile 0505-719-7788 Email sowadari@naver.com

BOSTON SUNDAY HERALD
VINTAGE PAPER DOLLS

Published by Cow & Bridge Publishing Co.
First original image published by Boston Sunday Herald 1895
This recovering edition published by Cow & Bridge Publishing Co. Korea

이 책의 저작권 및 출판권은 도서출판 소와다리가 소유하며 무단복제를 금합니다.

1판 1쇄 2015년 4월 20일
지은이 보스톤 선데이 헤럴드
발행인 김동근
발행처 소와다리
주소 인천광역시 남구 구월로 40번길 6-21번지 3가동 302호
대표전화 0505-719-7787
팩시밀리 0505-719-7788
출판등록 제2011-000015호(2011년 8월 3일)
이메일 sowadari@naver.com
ISBN 978-89-98046-56-9 (14690)

※잘못 만들어진 책은 구입하신 서점을 통해 바꾸어드립니다.

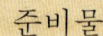

준비물

인형과 옷을 대충 오려낼 잘 드는 가위

세밀한 부분을 잘라낼 커터칼

칼질할 때 깔고 할 커팅패드 또는 두꺼운 종이

그 밖에 스카치테이프, 딱풀, 자 등등

받침대

실선을 따라 오린 후

점선을 접으면 받침대가 됩니다.

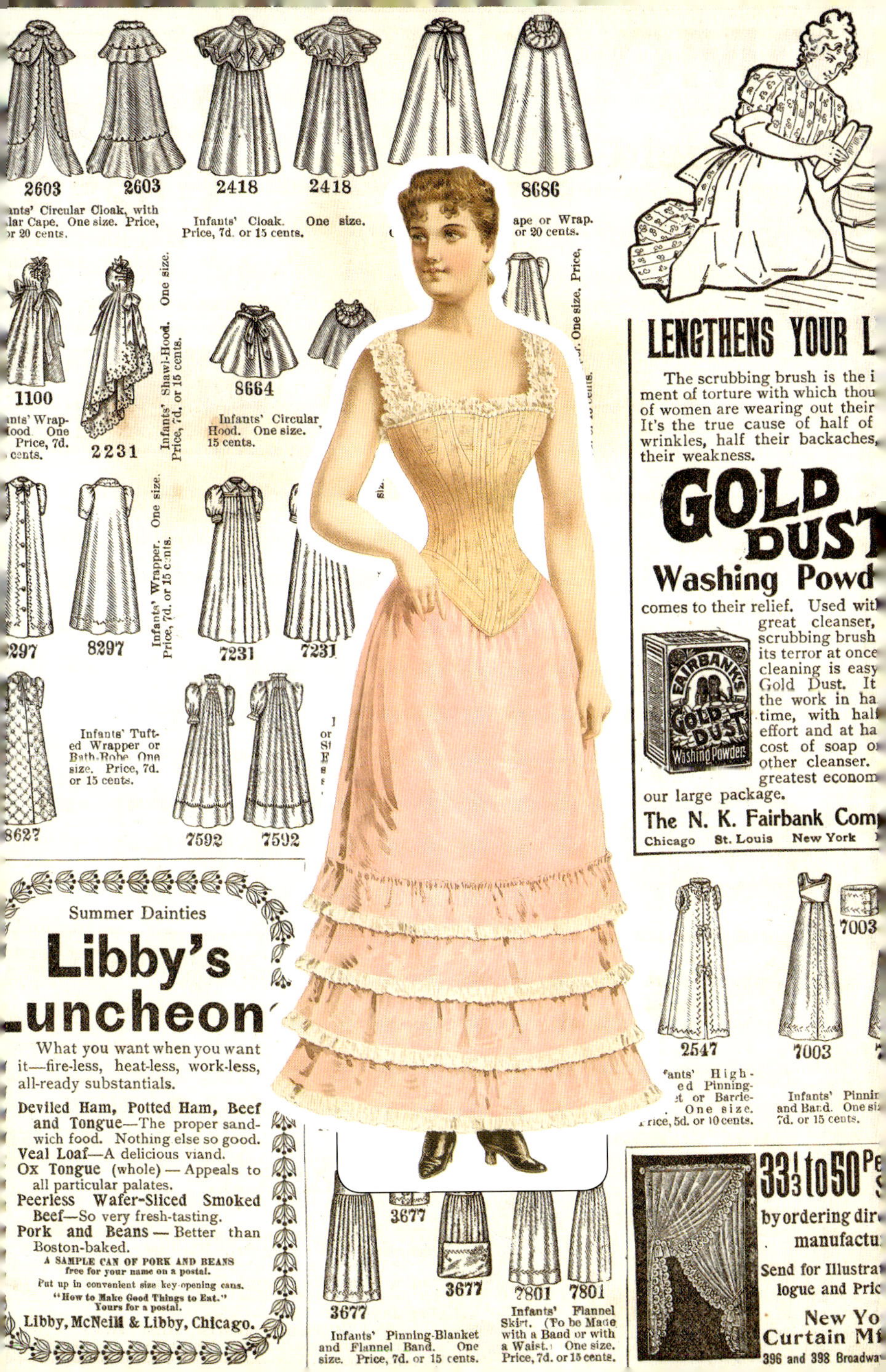

2603 **2603**
Infants' Circular Cloak, with lar Cape. One size. Price, r 20 cents.

2418 **2418**
Infants' Cloak. One size. Price, 7d. or 15 cents.

8686
ape or Wrap. or 20 cents.

1100
ood One food Price, 7d. ents.

2231

Infants' Shaw-Hood. One size. Price, 7d. or 15 cents.

8664

Infants' Circular Hood. 15 cents.

297 **8297**

Infants' Wrapper. One size. Price, 7d. or 15 cents.

7231 **7231**

8627

Infants' Tuft-ed Wrapper or Bath-Robe. One size. Price, 7d. or 15 cents.

7592 **7592**

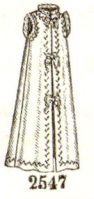
2547

ants' High-ed Pinning-t or Barde-One size. rice, 5d. or 10 cents.

7003

7003

Infants' Pinnin and Band. One siz 7d. or 15 cents.

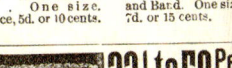

3677

3677

3677

Infants' Pinning-Blanket and Flannel Band. One size. Price, 7d. or 15 cents.

7801 **7801**

Infants' Flannel Skirt. (To be Made with a Band or with a Waist.) One size. Price, 7d. or 15 cents.

THE PRESIDENTS OF THE UNITED STATES AND DECLARATION OF INDEPENDENCE

THOMAS JEFFERSON.

JOHN ADAMS.

JAMES MADISON.

JAMES MONROE.

JOHN Q. ADAMS.

ANDREW JACKSON.

MARTIN VAN BUREN.

W. H. HARRISON.

JOHN TYLER.

JAMES K. POLK.

THE CAPITOL.

PRESIDENTS HOUSE.

TO THE MOST
HIGH AND MIGHTIE

Prince, I A ~~MES~~ of God

King

THE TR ~~~~ BLE
wish G

Rare Bk Room
99
Wm C. Hollands
4-29-36

Reat ings (most dread
Soue OD, the Father
of a s the people of
GER your Maiesties
y e ouer vs. For
of many, who
that vpon the
~~~~arre Queene
morie, some
thicke and palpable erfhadowed
this land, that mer hey were to
walke, and that it f he vnfetled
State: the appear s ftrength,
inftantly difpell vnto all
that were well n we be-
held the go hope-
full Seede Peace
and tranqui

But amongft r hearts,
then the bleffed continua s facred word a-
mongft vs, which is that ineftimable treafure, which excelleth all the riches
of the earth, becaufe the fruit thereof extendeth it felfe, not onely to the time
fpent in this tranfitory world, but directeth and difpofeth men vnto that E-
ternall happineffe which is aboue in Heauen.

Then, not to fuffer this to fall to the ground, but rather to take it vp, and
to continue it in that State, wherein the famous predeceffour of your HIGH-
NESSE did leaue it; Nay, to goe forward with the confidence and refo-
lution

Dress 9325
Transfer 2355

Blouse 9132
Skirt 9339
Transfer 10473

Dress 932
Transfer 235

MANAGED WITH COSTUMES LIKE THESE

STYLES IN COATS AND FROCKS

FIGURE NO. 1.

FIGURE NO.

No. 5.

FIGURE NO. 3.

**FANCY BLOUSES
and WAISTS.**

(For Patterns, Descriptions, etc., see
Pages 524 and 525.)

owder and Talcum Holder.
This beautiful imported toilet container is made of fancy design with gilt screw top and patent knob sifter attachment. The beautifully blended colors make it handsome and no cut can do justice to this article. Just the thing for holding your face powders or talcums and can be closed to prevent sifting. Every lady or gentleman should have in assorted colors. Retail
182 Price, per box, 47c
y Glass Puff Box.
187 Our price......28c
ted Glass Puff Box.
Beautiful Bohemian glass, assorted colors, fancy metallic clasp. Top of box of elaborate design. A very beautiful puff box.
No. 8F3189 Price...... 37c
wder Leaves for the Complexion.
Feuilles Poudrées
oated side over the face or moves dust and oily secrehe surface of the skin, giveautifully soft, velvet like and producing a cool, reling. An examination of fter using will show how the removed the oil and dust, e of the old style puff were ered. Ladies will find it can be conveniently carried cet, hand or traveling bag, not soil the dress with powdsome mirror is attached k. Gentlemen prefer to use ing, especially when travel-
191 Price, per book, contains 50 leaves..........20c
Book Toilet Case.
Handy Little Toilet Case. Appeals to every woman. Small silver plated box, hinged cover with mirror within, small down puff with handle. Being small enough to ket book, is just the article traveling, etc. Regular
193 Price 18c
ndy Toilet Box.
round old box design, round or, and box, is overed, nported der. This article is especially imported by us from France. A toilet set for traveling.
195 Price.........21c
Rouge de Theatre.
ROUGE DE THEATRE Ed. Pica & Cie. PARIS
This is positively the best, giving a natural and lifelike glow, never injures the skin, is today considered by the theatrical profession the only safe and satisfactory rouge, and used by them almost exclusively owing to the fine distributive qualities which it possesses so that it can never be noticed or detected.
No. 8F3197 Price, per box.......12c
If by mail, postage extra, per box, 6 cents.
Liquid Rouge.
A harmless liquid preparation for giving color to cheeks and lips. Makes them a perfectly pretty color.
jority of ladies form, as it is put ient manner and
No. 8F3202
If by mail, po
Eye Brow
For darkening the eye brows and lashes. The ge pencils. Unsurpassed ening the eye brows manner so natural th tected. Absolutely ly used by theatrica out the beauty of whether brown or bl
No. 8F3205 cents; our price Postage ext
Camphor
CAMPHORACEOUS COLD CREAM SEROCO
soothing burns, the skin No. If by
cures of the hair falling out, and all troubles of the scalp and hair. Will positively clear the scalp from dandruff and render it healthy, promoting the growth of the hair. Its life producing properties cause the hair to grow quickly, long, healthy and beautiful. It is recommended to ladies who desire long, glossy hair. It keeps the hair soft and silky; prevents baldness. You will see improvement in the first few applications.
No. 8F3210 Price, per bottle....34c
Unmailable on account of weight.
Hair Elixir.
MAGIC HAIR ELIXIR SEARS, ROEBUCK CHICAGO ILL.
A beautiful dressing for the hair, making it soft and fluffy; prevents it from splitting and falling out. Cures dandruff and makes the hair grow. Our Hair Elixir is used and recommended by every professional hair dresser in large cities. It is the only safe hair preserver known, and should be used especially for protecting and promoting a fine growth of hair.
No. 8 Price, per 8-ounce bottle..........45c
Unma account of weight.
inine Hair Tonic.
of the ottles....35c d tube extra, unmailable
pers' Egg ampoo.
mpoo is the highf shampoo prepsed by the first rs in the large very popular in the country. an's shampoo it makes clean hair, removes he scalp, and is not to contain, ther egg shamkali, which leaves and dry. Our g Shampoo rendr soft, smooth
6 Price, 8-oz. bottle....25c account of ht.
La Dore's Hair Powder.
LADORE'S HAIR POWDER
Will clean the hair, remove all oil, is an absorbent and will keep the hair dry and fluffy without the use of water. The powder absorbs the oil from the hair, leaving it soft and glossy and at the same time leaves the oil at the roots where it is required to give life and nourishment to the hair. Easy to apply, easily removed and very effective. Saves washing the hair so often, which is injurious.
Pomade Phi
POMADE PHILACOME
An e ing fo musta fumed qualit large top bo venien ing ap pomad to any usuall and e bottle.
No. 8F3222 Pom Price, 2-ounce screw t
If by mail, postage
Olive Wax Pomatu
For fixing and la the hair, whiskers mustache. Highly fumed, each stick wra in tin foil.
No. 8F3224 Price, stick.........
If by mail, postage e 4 cents.
French Cos
Wrapped in foil; white. Retail price, to state kind wanted.
No. 8F3226 Price,
Magnesium C
MAGNESIA ALBA
Styptic Pe
STYPTIC PE
Used at shaving. stop bleeding. Should by everyone shaving
No. 8F3228 Price,
If by mail, postage
Hair C
CURLING FLUID SEROCO
This p keep th during t warmest harmless direction
No. 8F bottle.
If by ma mailin
Blondi
The Famous Ha Bleach. This is a pe fectly harmless pre aration that will grad ally turn the hair fro ny color to a beautif londe color. A hade of color can obtained, from lig brown to golden by f lowing the simple structions which go w each bottle. We guara tee that no harm to t hair will result in usi it, but rather it is clean ing and strengthenin
No. 8F3232 Price, bottle, 4 ounce capacit
No. 8F3233 Price, la
If by mail, postage a extra, small, 16 c unmailable on of weigh
REMEMB
We Can Save You Suit of Clo

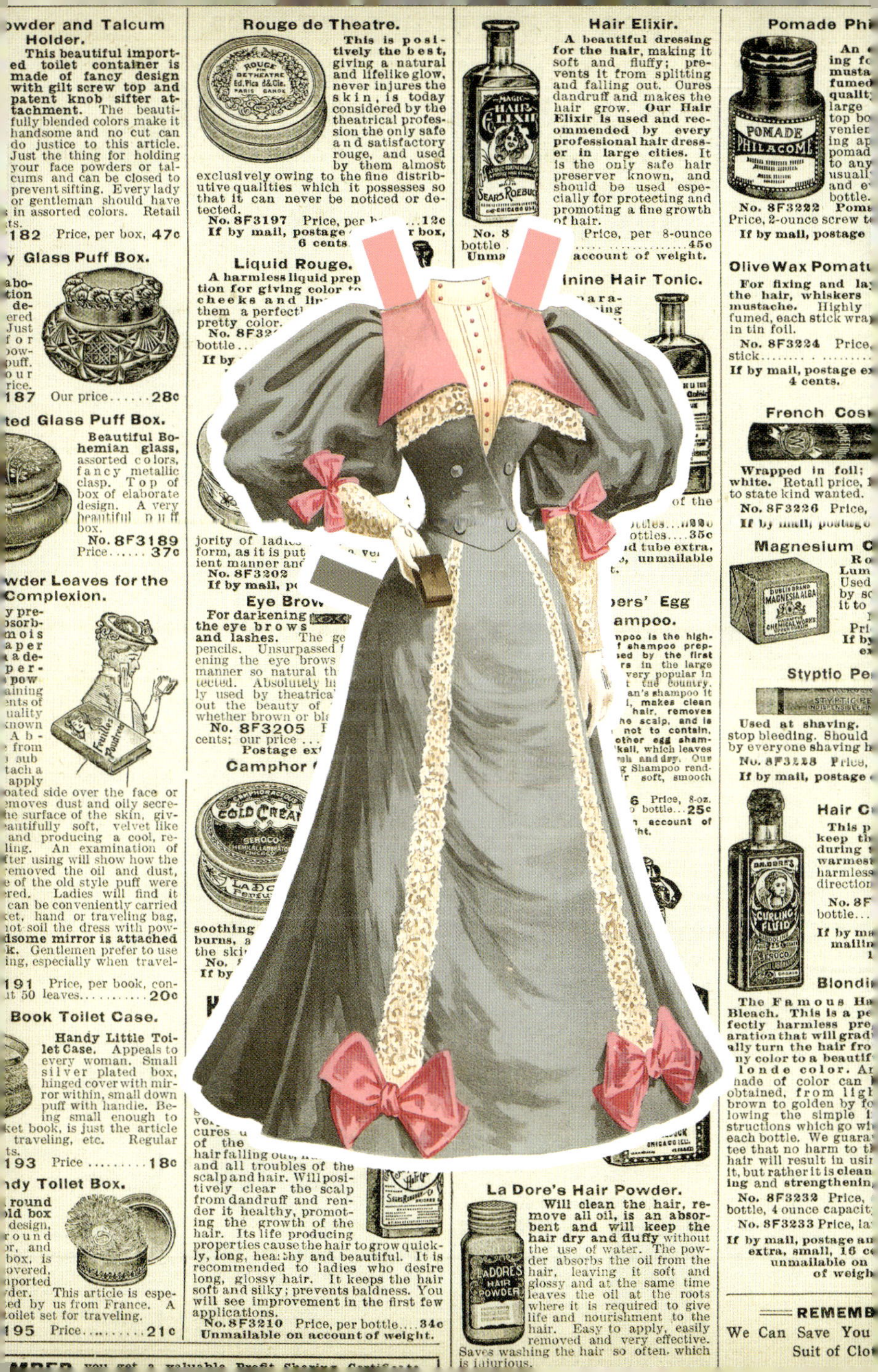

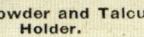

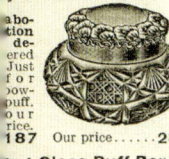

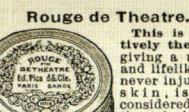

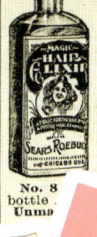

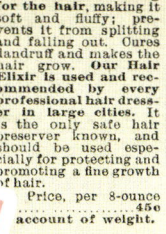

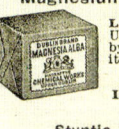

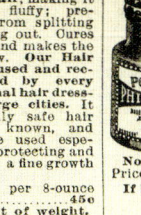

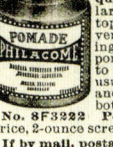

UNDERPINNINGS
OF PARIS

AN UNDERWORLD OF LACE
AND LINGERIE REVEALED BY
DOUCET, PREMET AND JENNY

*ale pink voile, pale silver-blue ribbons, and po
t embroidered with bouquets and baskets
Premet's offerings for a bridal set*

*If you look clo
distinguish th
Premet's embr
doves holding
of roses. The
flight across e
linen-thread la
with Turkish k
and Valenci*

*Jenny recognizes no
conventions in color
for her lingerie. This
combination is made
of sulphur-yellow
"gaze" trimmed with
lace*

*Flowered muslin in a
quite indescribable
design of white flow-
ers outlined with pink
on a blue ground, is
used by Jenny for her
box-plaited chemise*

*How far the little candle throws
its beam over Doucet's peignoir
of pink voile, girdled with tiny
flat roses made also of voile.
The design of the lace insertion
is delicately outlined in pink*

*An understudy for the one-piece
dress is Premet's one-piece-petti-
coat combination of pink voile
and sky-blue ribbons. The kilted
skirt is not left to its own devices,
but is held in by a blue ribbon*

*One of the best reasons for going
to bed is Doucet's plaited night-*

*For a tailored costume Doucet
makes a slip of beige chiffon a*

Y CHOCOLATE TOP.

No. 15L4048

$1.84

PER PAIR

BE SURE TO
STATE SIZE.

ce stay are cut
grade of chrome
leather. It is
very shapely last
quality sole and
Sizes and half
. Widths, D, E
ght, 28 ounces.

ELSIE.

No   16

0

IR

ROSALIE.

No. 15L4017

$2.25

PER PAIR

E TO
ZE.

della Diamond Tip Oxford, made from t...
perforated and Goodyear welt sewn. ...
aces are high foot fitting tongue so...
Made in the Blucher style with thre...
ad as beautiful a design as the most f...
wish for. Sizes and half sizes, 2½ to ...
E. Weight, 23 ounces.

THE COR...

PER PAIR

SURE TO
TE SIZE.

a choice selection of fine light weight
ltskin, with a collar and lace stay of
d. This is a dress shoe, made up without
h is the style especially used for evening
is made with great durability, so that it
egular every day wear just as well as heavier
es. It is high grade in every particular.
ial and workmanship, and quoted from 50

CAL...
BEA...

No. 15...

$1.

PER

BE SURE TO
STATE SIZE.

popular shoe with the ladies,
t coltskin, with golden brown kid
ucher style, neatly perforated and a
hoe at an uncommonly low figure.
izes, 2½ to 8.   Widths, C, D, E
t, 28 ounces.

BUC...
PRI...

No.

$1.

in this Ladies' Tan B...
tan buttons, perforate...
e buckle not only le...
be adjusted to cor...
fit as snug and t...
8.   Widths, C, D

OLDEN...
LASS...

No.

$1.

BE SURE TO
STATE SIZE.

$1.49

PER PAIR

The most
stylish and
serviceable
Misses' and
Children's Ox-
ford we carry.
Made of fine pat-
ent coltskin per-
forated tip and
laces, is genuine
fashionable and
serviceable
footwear. Sizes

BE SURE TO
STATE SIZE.

smooth dull calf top. Has ribbon
Goodyear welt sewn and just as
serviceable as our ladies' high grade

over. Is Goodyear welt sewn, carries
outside backstay, perforated tip and is
most comfortable natural last. This is
brown leather you have read so much a...

New and Exclusive
Designs in

China Closets

At Specia
gain Pr

HE PRICES at which these magnificent, solid quarter sawed oak China closets
are offered are genuine bargain prices as compared with prices charged
others for China Closets of the similar make and quality. Having received from the
anufacturer extremely favorable terms on the strength of an enormously large contract,
are in a position to give far greater intrinsic values than have ever before been at-
npted. We take the liberty therefore, to urge upon you, that if you are in need of a
ina closet and want to effect a large saving, want to get the biggest value possible for
ery dollar you pay, choose one of these magnific china closets. ur prices and
ms, under our iron clad guarantee to satisfy return your we feel that
are making inducements that you cannot af verlook. W of no other
use which offers you such broad and liberal tre and we at any time
demonstrate that we carry out our promises. S will send you
handsomest, best made, lowest priced cabinet Colonial

HE CHINA CLOSET HEREWITH full,
ble strength glass front, a plain but l,
ge, genuine French bevel plate mi It
vy hand carving of a neat patter.
71 inches high and 39 inches wide
lly grained solid oak.

HE CABINET is solid oa
the door
rk is beautifully figured quarte
in oak. The finish is very elab
mirror like smoothness. The ill
totally inadequate to properly cor
is impossible to show anything bu
in of the wood, the handsome shad et
ship it to you, set it up in your hom s to
a genuine Spiegel, May, Stern bar

HE WORKMANSHIP in this had.
ys only the most expert cabinet mak em-ct.
the reputation of the manufacturer is de
ds. Like ourselves, he has built up si-
ely not tolerate an imperfect piece of t er abmn
ket to a china closet, take our advice and ment
to your approval. Send us your order may
the cabinet will be sent you immediate ggest
it and decide whether or not you wish t 15 to
again you ever saw, a better cabinet than e may
% more money, we would consider it a fa hipped
nd your money together with all tra
ect from factory in S thern Indiana.
. H-5946. Price ....

some pattern and is 24 inches long and 8 inches high.

$13.9

ina Closet $1

one of the best values
ered. It will truly be a
r any dining room and
25% to 40% of our price.
carved claw foot and French
irror top, set off as it is with
an illustration. It must be se
on our 30 day free trial off
re than we say of it, you ma
paying for it.

NA CLOSET is ma
selecte
olished. It is 72 inches hig
s made by skilled cabinet
al construction throughou
ng position. The accomp
ful cabinet, as it is posi
er been made. The beautif
beveled plate mirror in the c

.95

THE FRONT COLUMNS, standing as they do away fro
this case, are of a most pleas
are two inches in diameter and extend from the top shelf to the base
handsome French legs are fastened. The full round effect in the chin
is made possible by using bent glass in the doors, and adds wonderfully
ance of this china closet.

ORDER THIS PIECE TODAY. Do not overlook t
value if you are con
purchase of a china closet. Simply send us a small payment, the amoun
be found by referring to page 12, and we will ship it to you without de
your approval. It is shipped from factory in Southern Indiana and is

$16.55

2603 **2603**
nts' Circular Cloak, with
ar Cape. One size. Price,
20 cents.

2418 **2418**
Infants' Cloak. One si
Price, 7d. or 15 cents.

8686 **8686**
Infants' Circular Ca__rap.
__ size. Price, 10d. __

1100
ts' Wrap-
ood. One
Price, 7d.
nts.

2231
Infants' Shawl-Hood.
Price, 7d. or 15 cents.

Infants' Wrapper. One size.
Price, 7d. or 15 cents.

One size.

__, Price,

297 **8297**

7231

627
Infants' Tuft-
ed Wrapper or
Bath Robe. One
size. Price, 7d.
or 15 cents.

7592

7003

7003

g-
rie-
size.
10 cents.

Infants' Pinning
and Band. One siz
7d. or 15 cents.

3677
3677
3677
Infants' Pinning-Blanket
and Flannel Band. One
size. Price, 7d. or 15 cents.

2801 **7801**
Infants' Flannel
Skirt. (To be Made
with a Band or with
a Waist.) One size.
Price, 7d. or 15 cents.

FIGURE No. 1.

FIGURE No. 2

FIGURE No. 3.

No. 4.

No. 5.

6.

**FANCY BLOUSES
and WAISTS.**

(For Patterns, Descriptions, etc., see
Pages 524 and 525.)

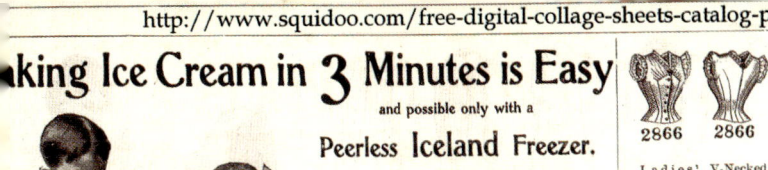

king Ice Cream in **3** Minutes is Easy

and possible only with a

Peerless Iceland Freezer.

It makes Ice Cream and dozens of delicious
frozen dainties—*better—easier—quicker*—
and *chea* — 'han any you can — because
it is   lest, and costs r   han a
poor o   ite today for   oklet,
"Ice C

The Third Minute."   Address Department C   D.

2866   2866   2903   29

Ladies' V-Necked
Corset-Cover, with Frill
Sleeves, 30 to 46 inches
bust, 9 sizes. Price, 7d.
or 15 cents.

Ladies' Pompado
set -Cover, the 9a
which may be in
Pompadour shape.
46 inches bust, 9.
Price, 7d. or 15 cen

1   8701   4636   46

Corset-Cover.
nches bust, 13
ce, 10d. or 20

Ladies' Corset
30 to 46 inches b
sizes. Price, 10d.
cents.

1673   1673   4654   46

Ladies' Seamless Cor-
set-Cover, 30 to 46 inches
bust, 9 sizes. Price, 7d.
or 15 cents.

Ladies' Corset
30 to 46 inches b
sizes. Price, 10d.
cents.

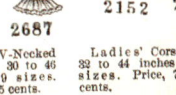

2687   2152   2

V-Necked
r. 30 to 46
t, 9 sizes.
or 15 cents.

Ladies' Corset
32 to 44 inches
sizes. Price, 7d
cents.

GD CHICAGO WAI

ice **$1.00**

v fitted with our
ed attachment for
upporters—appre
by every woman
vears
pin-
un-
of
D-
his
s t
t.

Try It.

Made of fine
sateen, fast
black, drab
or white;
clasp or button front; sizes, 18
waist measure.

Ask your dealer for the **G-D Chicago Wa**
If he hasn't it, send $1.00 money-order or sta
mentioning color and size desired, and we will send
one, prepaid.

GAGE-DOWNS CO., 268 Fifth Ave., Chica

**1566   1479   L
wit
Yo
4f**

adies' Sack Chem-
with Round or
are Neck. 28 to
inches bust, 10
s. Price, 10d. or
ents.

Ladies' Sack
Chemise, Fastened
on the Shoulders.
30 to 46 inches bust,
9 sizes. Price, 10d.
or 20 cents.

7380   7380

adies' Combination Corset
ver or Chemise and Clos
awers. (To be Made wit'
zh or Low Neck, with or v
Sleeves and with the Dra
in at the Knee or Finis
h a Band.) 28 to 50 inches
st, 15 sizes Price, 1s. 3d. or
cents.

15 sizes.
30 cents.

1199   4660   4660   4658   4658   4661

adies' Medium-
ade Drawers, with
kc. (Closed at the
es,) 20 to 36 inches
aist, 9 sizes. Price,
1, or 20 cents.

Ladies' Open Drawers,
with Pointed Front-Yoke.
20 to 36 inches waist, 9
sizes. Price, 10d or 20
cents.

Ladies' Open Drawers,
Lapped at the Back. 20 to
36 inches waist, 9 sizes.
Price, 10d. or 20 cents.

Ladies' Drawers,
Buttoned at the Sides.
20 to 36 inches waist,
9 sizes. Price, 10d.
or 20 cents.

AGE OF NOVELTY SHOES FOR WOMEN A
MISSES AT WORLD BEATING PRICES

Y CHOCOLATE TOP.

No. 15L4048

$1.84
PER PAIR

BE SURE TO
STATE SIZE.

ce stay are cut
grade of chrome
leather. It is
ery shapely last
quality sole and
Go
Sizes and half
Widths, D, E
ght, 28 ounces.

ELSIE.

No.

CAL
BEA

No. 1

BE SURE TO
STATE SIZE.

A popular shoe with the ladies,
patent coltskin, with golden brown kid
the Blucher style, neatly perforated and a
able shoe at an uncommonly low figure.
half sizes, 2½ to 8. Widths, C, D, E
Weight, 28 ounces.

ROSALIE.

No. 15L4017

$2.25
PER PAIR

LA

lla Diamond Tip Oxford, made from tan ca
forated and Goodyear welt sewn. Has
es and the high foot fitting tongue so por
ade in the Blucher style with three ey
as beautiful a design as the most fash
sh for. Sizes and half sizes, 2½ to 8.
Weight, 23 ounces.

THE CORI

PER P.

BUC
PRIN

No.

$1.

BE SURE TO
STATE SIZE.

st of the new in this Ladies' Tan Bu
calfskin with tan buttons. perforated
her style. The buckle not only len
hoe, but it can be adjusted to confe
aking the shoe fit as snug and clos
sizes, 2½ to 8. Widths, C, D,
ces.

$1.49
PER PAIR

GOLDEN B
LASSI

No.

$1.

PE

TO
E SIZE.

choice selection of fine light weight
kin, with a collar and lace stay of
is the style especially used for evening
made with great durability, so that it
lar every day wear just as well as heavier
It is high grade in every particular,
and workmanship, and quoted from 50

BE SURE TO
STATE SIZE.

smooth dull calf top. Has ribbon
Goodyear welt sewn and just as

The most
stylish and
serviceable
Misses' and
Children's Ox-
ford we carry.
Made of fine pat-
ent coltskin per-
forated tip and
laces, is genuine
fashionable and

BE SURE TO
STATE SIZE.

over. Is Goodyear welt sewn, carries a
outside backstay, perforated tip and is
most comfortable natural last. This is

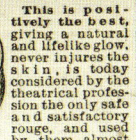
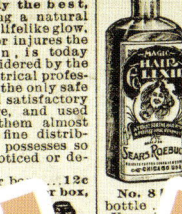

TO THE MOST
HIGH AN~~D~~ M~~IG~~HTIE

Prince, I A M~~ES~~ ~~by the grace~~ of God

Kin~~g~~

THE T~~ranslators of the Bib~~LE

with ~~Grace, Mercie, and Peace.~~

G~~reat~~ Rea~~d~~ ~~and gracious~~ ~~Ki~~ngs (most dread
Sou~~eraigne~~ ~~G~~o d, the Father
~~a~~s the people of
your Maiesties
~~pow~~ ouer vs. For
~~the zeale~~ of many, who
~~wish~~ that vpon the
~~setting vp of~~ ~~that~~ ~~st~~arre Queene
~~of me~~ ~~m~~orie, some
~~thicke clowdes of darkenesse which had ouer~~shadowed
this land, that me~~n were in doubt which way th~~ey were to
walke, and that it ~~should hardly be knowne who was to~~ ~~le~~ad
~~in~~ ~~the vn~~setled
State: the appea~~rance of your Maiestie, as of the~~ ~~Sun in his~~ strength,
instantly dispe~~lled those supposed and surmised mists, and gaue~~ ~~v~~nto all
that were wel ~~affected exceeding cause of comfort; especially when~~ we be-
held the go~~uernment established in your Highnesse, and your~~ ~~ho~~pe-
full Seede ~~by an vndoubted Title, and this also accompanied with~~ Peace
and tran~~quilitie, at home and abroad.~~

But am~~ong all our ioyes, there was no one that more filled our~~ ~~h~~earts,
then the bless~~ed continuance of the preaching of Gods sacr~~ed word a-
mongst vs, which is that ineftimable treafure, which excelleth all the riches
of the earth, becaufe the fruit thereof extendeth it felfe, not onely to the time
fpent in this tranfitory world, but directeth and difpofeth men vnto that E-
ternall happineffe which is aboue in Heauen.

Then, not to fuffer this to fall to the ground, but rather to take it vp, and
to continue it in that State, wherein the famous predeceffour of your HIGH-
NESSE did leaue it; Nay, to goe forward with the confidence and refo-
lution

A 2

받침대

실선을 따라 오린 후
점선을 접으면 받침대가 됩니다.

받침대

실선을 따라 오린 후
점선을 접으면 받침대가 됩니다.